# 101 Things To Do With Canned Biscuits

# 101 Things To Do With Canned Biscuits

BY
TONI PATRICK

GIBBS SMITH
TO ENRICH AND INSPIRE HUMANKIND

Published by
Gibbs Smith
P.O. Box 667
Layton, Utah 84041

1-800.835.4993 orders
www.gibbs-smith.com

Designed by Kurt Wahlner

Library of Congress Cataloging-in-Publication Data
Patrick, Toni.
101 things to do with canned biscuits / Toni Patrick.—1st ed.
p. cm.
ISBN-13: 978-1-4236-5688-3
1. Biscuits. I. Title. II. Title: One hundred one things to do with canned biscuits. III. Title: One hundred and one things to do with canned biscuits.
TX770.B55P38 2008
641.8'15—dc22
                    2008000114

To my family:
Thank you for your love and support. I could
not have done this without you!

All my love,
Toni

Yum!
www.gibbs-smith.com

# CONTENTS

## Helpful Hints 9

### Appetizers



### Breads



### Breakfast

# Lunch



# Dinner



# Desserts

# HELPFUL HINTS

1. All biscuits used in this cookbook are refrigerated canned biscuits.

2. Different brands of biscuits have different weight measurements. Choose the size nearest to what is listed in the recipe ingredient list. If you only have one size of biscuit  available, you can adjust most recipes. Jumbo biscuits can be split in half while still raw.

3. As a quick reference to make it easier for you to choose the correct size of biscuits, the below chart lists the weight measurement with the biscuit count per can for the sizes used in the recipes in this cookbook. The ingredient lists only show the weight measurements.

| 16.3 ounce can | 8 jumbo-size biscuits |
| 12 ounce can | 10 regular-size biscuits |
| 10 ounce can | 5 jumbo-size biscuits |
| 7 ounce can | 10 small-size biscuits |
| 6 ounce can | 5 regular-size biscuits |

4. Baking times may vary with different brands of biscuits. Refer to the package and adjust baking time accordingly. You should check the food near the end of the baking time to make sure it is cooking properly.

5. If a recipe calls for muffin cups and there are empty cups after preparing the food (for instance, you have a 12-cup muffin tin and the recipe uses only 10 cups) be sure to fill the empty cups half-full of water prior to baking. This will prevent uneven baking and damage to your muffin tin.

6. Most dishes can be made and then refrigerated prior to baking.

7. When flattening biscuits, it is easier to stretch the dough gradually around the edges, like with pizza dough, rather than using a rolling pin.

8. To reduce fat calories choose reduced-fat biscuits and skim milk. Low-fat ingredients, such as light soups, sour cream and cream cheese can be substituted.

9. 1 garlic clove equals 1 teaspoon minced garlic from the jar. Jarred garlic is much quicker and more cost effective.

10. $\frac{1}{4}$ cup fresh minced onion equals 2 tablespoons dried minced onion.

11. $\frac{1}{4}$ cup fresh herbs equals 1 tablespoon dried herbs.

12. Fresh or frozen vegetables, steamed, can be substituted for canned vegetables.

13. Be creative! Most ingredients can be adjusted to your own liking.

# APPETIZERS

# TURKEY EMPANADAS

| | |
|---:|:---|
| 1 pound | **ground turkey** |
| 1 | **large onion,** diced |
| 1 can (8 ounces) | **tomato sauce** |
| 4 teaspoons | **Cajun seasoning mix** |
| | **salt and pepper** |
| ½ cup | **grated Monterey Jack cheese** |
| 3 cans (7 ounce each) | **biscuits** |
| 1 | **egg,** beaten |
| | **oil,** for deep frying |

Saute turkey in large frying pan over medium heat until brown, breaking up meat with fork, about 5 minutes. Using slotted spoon, transfer turkey to small bowl. Add onion to drippings in frying pan and saute until light brown, about 7 minutes. Return turkey and any juices to frying pan. Add tomato sauce and Cajun seasoning; simmer until mixture is almost dry, stirring occasionally, about 8 minutes. Season with salt and pepper. Cool completely. Mix in cheese.

Flatten each biscuit into a 4-inch round. Place 1 tablespoon filling on round. Brush half of dough edge with egg. Fold dough over filling to create half circle and seal edges by pressing with tines of fork. Set empanada on baking sheet and cover with damp paper towel. Repeat with remaining biscuits and filling.

Pour oil to depth of ½ inch into heavy large frying pan. Heat oil over medium-high heat to 350 degrees. Fry empanadas in batches until golden brown, about 2 minutes per side. Transfer to a plate covered with paper towels. Serve warm or at room temperature. Makes 30 empanadas.

# WRAPPED SMOKIES WITH MUSTARD SAUCE

|  |  |
|---:|:---|
| 1 can (12 ounces) | **biscuits** |
| 10 | **little smoked sausages** |
| 2 tablespoons | **sugar** |
| 1 tablespoon | **dry mustard** |
| 2 tablespoons | **cornstarch** |
| 1/2 tablespoon | **garlic powder** |
| 1/2 tablespoon | **onion powder** |
| 1 can | **beer** |
| 1 tablespoon | **red wine vinegar** |

Preheat oven to 400 degrees.

Flatten each biscuit into a 6-inch round. Quarter biscuits and wrap around uncooked wieners. Roll and seal the edges, completely covering the wiener. Place on lightly greased baking sheet and bake for 10 minutes or until dough is golden brown.

In a medium saucepan, combine sugar, mustard, cornstarch, garlic powder, and onion powder. Cook on low heat until mixture combines, stirring constantly, about 1 minute. Add in beer and vinegar. Cook over medium heat, stirring constantly, until thickened. Serve as dipping sauce. Makes 10 servings.

# SPINACH ARTICHOKE DIP IN BREAD BOWLS

| | |
|---:|:---|
| 1 package (8 ounces) | **cream cheese** |
| 1/2 cup | **mayonnaise** |
| 2 packages (9 ounces each) | **frozen creamed spinach,** thawed |
| 1 can (14 ounces) | **artichoke hearts,** drained and chopped |
| 1/2 cup | **grated Parmesan cheese** |
| 1/3 cup | **chopped onion** |
| 1/8 teaspoon | **cayenne pepper** |
| 2 cans (16.3 ounces each) | **biscuits** |
| 1/3 cup | **crushed herbed stuffing** |
| 1/2 cup | **chopped pecans** |

Preheat oven to 375 degrees. Grease 16 muffin cups.

Combine cream cheese and mayonnaise in a large bowl. Stir in creamed spinach, artichokes, Parmesan cheese, onion, and pepper.

Flatten each biscuit into a 6-inch round. Place in muffin cups, pressing firmly into the bottom and up the sides of cup. Spoon dip evenly into each cup. Combine stuffing and pecans; sprinkle on top. Bake for 17–20 minutes or until biscuits are golden brown. Makes 16 servings.

# MEATBALL PUFFS

|  |  |
|---|---|
| 2 cans (16.3 ounces each) | **biscuits** |
| 16 | **frozen Italian meatballs,** thawed |
| ⅔ cup | **grated mozzarella cheese** |
| 1 cup | **marinara sauce** |

Preheat oven to 375 degrees.

Flatten each biscuit into a 5-inch round. Sprinkle with cheese and place a meatball in the center. Wrap dough around the meatball and pinch to seal. Place, pinched side down, on a slightly greased baking sheet. Bake for 17–20 minutes or until biscuits are golden brown. Serve warm with marinara sauce for dipping. Makes 16 servings.

# TASTY FLOWERS

|  |  |
|---|---|
| ¼ cup | **preserves,** flavor of choice |
| ¼ cup | **cream cheese** |
| 1 can (12 ounces) | **biscuits** |

Preheat oven according to package directions.

In a medium bowl blend preserves and cream cheese. Place biscuits on a lightly greased baking sheet. Make five slashes on each biscuit to form the petals. Make an indentation in the center of the biscuit and drop in a teaspoon of cream cheese mixture.

Bake according to package directions. Makes 10 servings.

# CHICKEN AND DUMPLINGS

|  |  |
|---|---|
| 3 cans (15 ounces each) | **chunky home-style chicken noodle soup** |
| 1 can (14 ounces) | **chicken or vegetable broth** |
| 1 can (12 ounces) | **biscuits** |

Combine soups in large pot and bring to a boil.

Cut each biscuit into fourths. Drop biscuits into boiling soup and cook uncovered for 10 minutes at a medium boil. Cover and continue to cook for another 10 minutes until biscuits are fluffy. Makes 8 servings.

# CHEESE BALLS

| | |
|---:|:---|
| 1 can (12 ounces) | **biscuits** |
| 6 ounces | **cheddar cheese,** cut into 40 cubes |
| 1/4 cup | **crushed cornflakes** |
| 1/4 cup | **grated Parmesan cheese** |
| 1/4 teaspoon | **garlic powder** |
| 1/3 cup | **butter,** melted |

Preheat oven to 400 degrees.

Cut each biscuit into fourths. Flatten each piece and place a cheese cube in to center. Wrap dough around cheese and seal with a pinch. Shape into a ball.

Combine cornflakes, cheese, and garlic powder. Roll each ball in butter then in cornflake mixture. Place on a lightly greased baking sheet. Bake for 7–9 minutes or until golden brown. Serve hot. Makes 40 balls.

# SHRIMP AND PORK POT STICKERS

| | |
|---|---|
| ¼ pound | **ground pork** |
| 1 can | **water chestnuts,** drained and diced |
| ½ pound | **shrimp,** peeled, deveined, and coarsely chopped |
| ¾ cup | **chopped scallions** |
| 1-½ tablespoons | **soy sauce** |
| 2 teaspoons | **minced fresh ginger** |
| 1 teaspoon | **Asian sesame oil** |
| 1 can (12 ounces) | **flaky biscuits** |
| ⅓ cup | **soy sauce** |
| 2 tablespoons | **Chinese vinegar** |
| 2 tablespoons | **water** |
| 1 teaspoon | **Asian chile oil** |
| ¼ cup | **peanut oil** |

In a medium frying pan, brown pork, stirring frequently to ensure pork is broken up into small pieces. Drain. In a large bowl, combine pork, chestnuts, shrimp, scallions, 1-½ tablespoons soy sauce, ginger, and sesame oil. Mix well.

Split biscuits in half by pulling apart at center layers. On a floured surface and using a floured rolling pin, flatten biscuits into 4-inch rounds. Cut each biscuit in half. Place a tablespoon of pork mixture on each half. Moisten edges with water and fold dough over mixture. Seal edges firmly with a fork. In a medium bowl, combine ⅓ cup soy sauce, vinegar, water, and chile oil to make dipping sauce.

Place peanut oil in a medium frying pan. Over medium heat, fry biscuits until lightly brown. Serve pot stickers warm with soy dipping sauce. Makes 40 pot stickers.

# COCKTAIL BISCUITS

Cream Cheese Spread:

| | |
|---:|:---|
| I package (8 ounces) | **cream cheese** |
| I-½ tablespoons | **half-and-half** |
| I teaspoon | **dill weed** |
| I clove | **garlic,** finely chopped |
| ¾ teaspoon | **chives** |
| ⅛ teaspoon | **hot sauce** |
| ⅛ teaspoon | **pepper** |
| ¼ teaspoon | **salt** |

Biscuits:

| | |
|---:|:---|
| 2 teaspoons | **butter** |
| I cup | **minced mushrooms** |
| 2 | **shallots,** minced |
| ½ cup | **inely chopped ham** |
| 2 | **green onions,** finely chopped |
| | **pepper,** to taste |
| I can (12 ounces) | **biscuits** |

In a large bowl, combine cream cheese and half-and-half; mix well. Add rest of ingredients for cream cheese spread and mix well. Place in refrigerator and chill overnight.

Preheat oven to 400 degrees.

In medium frying pan, melt butter and then saute mushrooms and shallots until tender. Add ham, onions, and pepper. Cook for 4 minutes. Remove from heat. Press each biscuit firmly into mushroom mixture coating the entire top of biscuit. Place on a lightly greased baking sheet. Make an indentation in each biscuit by pressing a tablespoon firmly in the center. Bake for 12–15 minutes. Top with cream cheese mixture. Makes 10 servings.

# ZUCCHINI AND CHEESE ROLL-UPS

| | |
|---:|:---|
| I cup | **chopped zucchini** |
| ¼ cup | **chopped onions** |
| I tablespoon | **butter** |
| ½ teaspoon | **dried dill weed** |
| ½ teaspoon | **basil** |
| I can (12 ounces) | **flaky biscuits** |
| I cup | **grated sharp cheddar cheese** |

Preheat oven to 400 degrees.

In a large frying pan, saute zucchini and onion in butter until tender. Remove from heat and stir in dill weed and basil.

Sprinkle flour on a large surface. Using a floured rolling pin, flatten biscuits into 5-inch rounds. Arrange biscuits so they are slightly over lapping, 2 across and 5 down. Flatten with the rolling pin to create a rectangle. Spread zucchini mixture evenly across biscuits and top with cheese.

Roll biscuits into a log beginning at the shortest edge and seal ends well. Cut into 10 pieces and place, cut side down, on a lightly greased baking sheet. Bake 15–20 minutes, until golden brown. Serve immediately. Makes 10 servings.

# BRUSCHETTA

|  |  |
|---|---|
| 1 cup | **olive oil** |
| ½ cup | **balsamic vinegar** |
| 1 teaspoon | **basil** |
| 1 teaspoon | **Dijon mustard** |
| 1 clove | **garlic,** minced |
| 6 large | **tomatoes,** sliced |
| 12 ounces | **pesto** |
| 6 ounces | **fresh mozzarella,** sliced |
| 1 can (12 ounces) | **flaky biscuits** |

Mix together oil, vinegar, basil, mustard, and garlic. Add tomatoes and place, covered, in refrigerator to marinate overnight.

Preheat oven to 400 degrees.

Cut biscuits in half horizontally. Flatten into 4-inch rounds and place on a greased baking sheet. Bake 10–15 minutes. Top each biscuit with pesto, tomato and mozzarella. Makes 20 servings.

# POTATO TURNOVERS

|            |                                         |
|-----------:|-----------------------------------------|
| 6 large | **potatoes,** peeled and cut in large pieces |
| 3 large | **onions,** finely diced |
| 3 tablespoons | **butter** |
| 2 cups | **grated cheddar cheese** |
| I can (12 ounces) | **flaky biscuits** |

In large pot, boil potatoes 20–25 minutes until soft. Drain.

Preheat oven to 400 degrees.

In a large frying pan, saute onions in butter until clear. Combine potatoes, onions, and cheese. With a hand mixer, blend until creamy.

On a lightly floured surface, flatten biscuits into 7-inch rounds using a floured rolling pin. Place 1/2 cup potato mixture in the center of each biscuit. Moisten edges with water and fold into half circles. Use fork to seal edges. Bake for 15 minutes or until lightly golden. Makes 10 servings.

# JALAPENO PUFFERS

1 can (12 ounces) **biscuits**  
10 slices **jalapeno**  
½ cup **grated cheddar cheese**

Preheat oven to 375 degrees.

Flatten each biscuit into a 5-inch round. Place a slice of jalapeno and a large pinch of cheddar cheese in the center of each biscuit. Fold biscuit over and pinch to seal edges. Place seam down on a lightly greased baking sheet. Bake until golden brown, about 15 minutes. Makes 10 servings.

# CHEESE CRESCENTS

|              |                              |
|-------------:|:-----------------------------|
| 2 tablespoons | **butter** |
| 2 teaspoons | **garlic powder** |
| ½ cup | **grated sharp cheddar cheese** |
| ½ cup | **grated mozzarella** |
| 1 can (12 ounces) | **biscuits** |

Preheat oven to 375 degrees.

Melt butter and add garlic powder. In a separate bowl, mix cheeses.

Flatten each biscuit into a 6-inch round and cut in half. Brush top of biscuit with garlic butter. Top with cheese blend. Beginning at the narrowest point, roll biscuit into a crescent. Drizzle butter over top. Place on a lightly greased baking sheet and bake for 15 minutes. Makes 20 crescents.

# PEPPERONI BITES

| | |
|---:|:---|
| I cup | **grated mozzarella cheese** |
| ½ cup | **chopped pepperoni** |
| ½ cup | **pizza sauce** |
| 2 cans (7 ounces each) | **biscuits** |
| I tablespoon | **milk** |
| ¼ cup | **grated Parmesan cheese** |
| I teaspoon | **oregano** |
| I teaspoon | **basil** |

Preheat oven to 350 degrees.

In a bowl, combine mozzarella cheese, pepperoni, and sauce. Set aside.

Flatten each biscuit into a 3-inch round. Place about I rounded teaspoon filling in the center of each circle. Bring edges of dough together. Pinch to seal. Place, seam side down, on greased baking sheets. Brush with milk. Sprinkle with Parmesan cheese, oregano and basil. Bake for 12–15 minutes or until golden brown. Makes 20 pieces.

# FETA BISCUITS

|  |  |
|---:|:---|
| ¾ cup | **crumbled feta cheese** |
| I tablespoon | **lemon juice** |
| I tablespoon | **dill** |
| I | **green onion,** finely chopped |
| I can (7 ounces) | **biscuits** |
| 10 | **green olives with pimientos** |

Preheat oven to 400 degrees.

In small serving bowl, combine cheese, lemon juice, dill, and onion.

Lightly grease 10 muffin cups. Cut each biscuit in half horizontally and arrange I layer in bottom of each muffin cup.

Place cheese mixture evenly among cups. Place one olive in the center of each. Top with remaining biscuit layer; press around edge of each biscuit to seal. Bake 8–10 minutes or until biscuits are golden brown. Let biscuits cool before serving. Makes 10 servings.

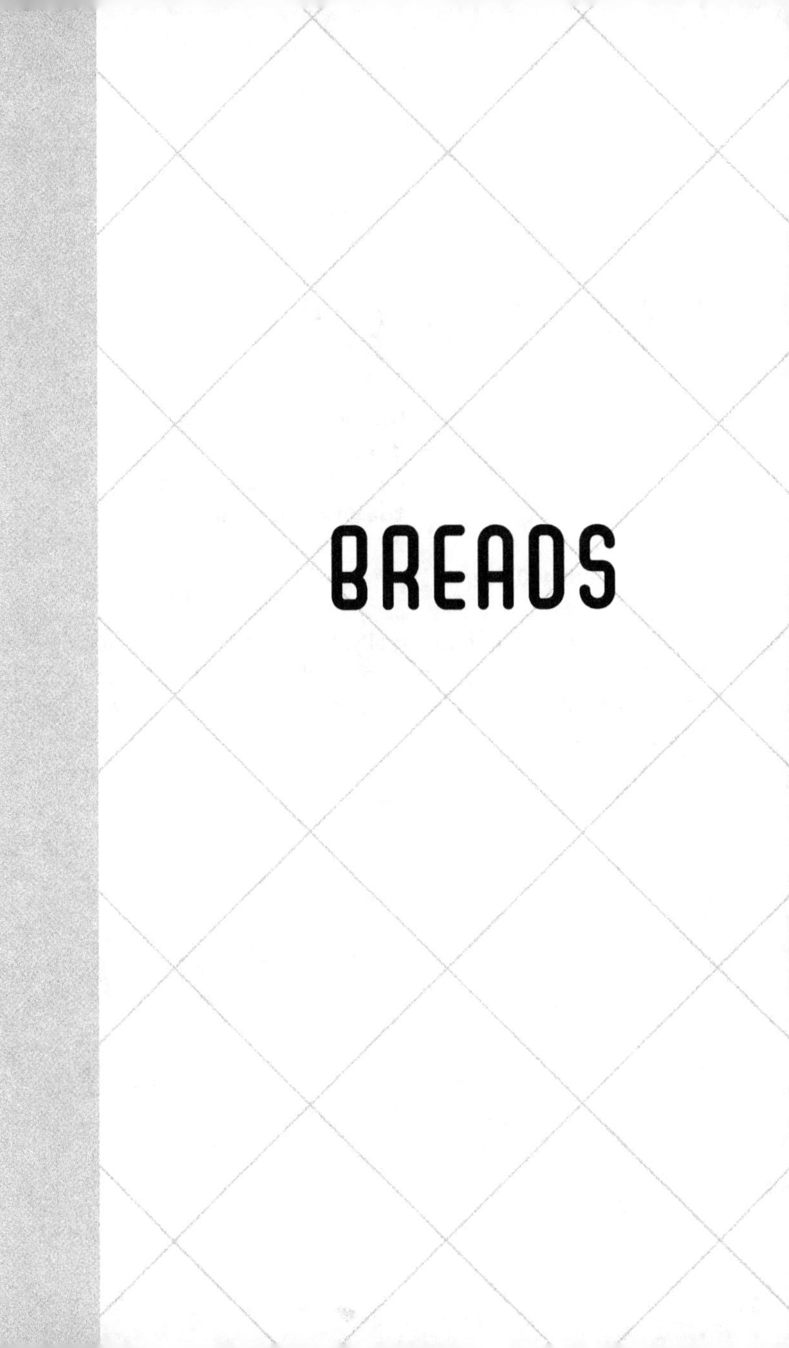
BREADS

# FOCACCIA BREAD

| | |
|---|---|
| I can (16.3 ounces) | **buttermilk biscuits** |
| ½ cup | **pesto** |
| ¼ cup | **grated Parmesan cheese** |
| ¼ cup | **toasted pine nuts** |

Preheat oven to 400 degrees.

Cut each biscuit in half horizontally. Flatten into 5-inch rounds. Place on lightly greased baking sheet. Top each with pesto, cheese, and pine nuts. Bake for 8–10 minutes or until edges are golden brown. Makes 16 servings.

# ITALIAN STYLE FLATBREAD

| | |
|---:|:---|
| ⅓ cup | **mayonnaise** |
| ⅓ cup | **grated Parmesan cheese** |
| ¼ teaspoon | **basil** |
| ¼ teaspoon | **oregano** |
| 3 | **green onions,** thinly sliced |
| 1 teaspoon | **minced garlic** |
| 1 can (12 ounces) | **biscuits** |
| ½ cup | **grated mozzarella cheese** |

Preheat oven to 400 degrees.

Combine mayonnaise, Parmesan cheese, basil, oregano, onions, and garlic.

Cut each biscuit in half horizontally. Flatten into 5-inch rounds. Place on a lightly greased baking sheet. Spread mixture over each biscuit. Top with mozzarella cheese. Bake 10–15 minutes or until biscuits are golden brown. Makes 20 servings.

# CHEESY PULL-APART BREAD

| | |
|---:|:---|
| I teaspoon | **garlic powder** |
| ¼ cup | **butter,** melted |
| ½ teaspoon | **dry mustard** |
| I can (16.3 ounces) | **biscuits** |
| ¼ cup | **grated Parmesan cheese** |

Preheat oven to 375 degrees.

Combine garlic, butter, and mustard in a bowl.

Cut each biscuit into fourths. Coat the bottom of a loaf pan with 2 tablespoons of the butter mixture. Dip each biscuit piece in butter mixture and place in bread pan. Drizzle remaining butter over top of biscuit pieces and top with cheese. Bake 30–40 minutes or until golden brown. Makes 10 servings.

# BUBBLE RING

|  |  |
|---:|:---|
| 8 slices | **bacon,** fried and crumbled |
| ½ cup | **grated Parmesan cheese** |
| ¼ cup | **diced green bell pepper** |
| ¼ cup | **diced onion** |
| I can (16.3 ounces) | **flaky biscuits** |
| ¼ cup | **butter,** melted |

Preheat oven to 350 degrees.

Combine bacon, cheese, pepper, and onion in a large bowl. Cut each biscuit into fourths. Place pieces in the bowl and toss to mix. Distribute mixture evenly in a lightly greased bundt pan. Bake for 20–30 minutes or until biscuits are golden brown. Makes I0 servings.

# CHEESE-TOPPED BISCUITS

| | |
|---:|:---|
| 2 cans (7 ounces each) | **biscuits** |
| 1 cup | **grated sharp cheddar cheese** |
| 2 tablespoons | **light cream** |
| ½ teaspoon | **poppy seeds** |
| dash | **dry mustard** |

Preheat oven to 425 degrees.

Arrange 15 biscuits, overlapping, around outside of a 9-inch round cake pan. Arrange remaining biscuits to make inner circle. Combine cheese, cream, poppy seeds, and mustard. Crumble evenly over top of biscuits. Bake 12–17 minutes. Remove from pan immediately and serve hot. Makes 8–10 servings.

# POPPY-ONION LOAF

|  |  |
|---:|:---|
| ¼ cup | **butter,** melted |
| 2 tablespoons | **onion flakes** |
| 1 tablespoon | **poppy seeds** |
| 1 can (16 ounces) | **buttermilk biscuits** |

Preheat oven to 350 degrees.

Stir together butter, onion, and poppy seeds.

Dip each biscuit into butter mixture, turning to coat. Arrange biscuits, standing on edge, in two rows in a 9 x 5-inch loaf pan. Brush with remaining butter mixture. Bake for 25–30 minutes or until golden brown. Let cool in pan for 10 minutes. Makes 10 servings.

# GARLIC BREAD

|  |  |
|---|---|
| ½ cup | **butter** |
| ¼ cup | **grated Parmesan cheese** |
| ½ teaspoon | **oregano** |
| 1 teaspoon | **garlic** |
| 3 cans (7 ounces each) | **biscuits** |

Preheat oven to 350 degrees.

Melt butter in bundt pan. Sprinkle with cheese, oregano, and garlic.

Open cans of biscuits and place in bundt pan, without separating biscuits. Bake 30–35 minutes. Invert onto a serving plate or wire rack. Makes 10–15 servings.

# HERBED BISCUIT STRIPS

<table>
<tr><td align="right">I can (16.3 ounces)</td><td>biscuits</td></tr>
<tr><td align="right">¼ cup</td><td>unsalted butter, melted</td></tr>
<tr><td align="right">I ½ teaspoon</td><td>Italian seasoning</td></tr>
<tr><td align="right">¼ teaspoon</td><td>paprika</td></tr>
<tr><td align="right">⅓ cup</td><td>grated Parmesan cheese</td></tr>
</table>

Preheat oven to 400 degrees.

Cut each biscuit into 4 strips.

Pour melted butter in a 9 x 9-inch pan. Sprinkle in Italian seasoning, paprika, and cheese. Place biscuit strips evenly on top of butter. Bake 15–20 minutes or until golden brown. Re-cut strips and serve. Makes 8–10 servings.

# CINNAMON NUT BISCUITS

| | |
|---|---|
| I can (16.3 ounces) | **flaky biscuits** |
| 3 tablespoons | **butter,** melted |
| ½ cup | **brown sugar** |
| ¾ teaspoon | **cinnamon** |
| ¼ cup | **chopped pecans** |

Preheat oven to 375 degrees.

Cut each biscuit in half horizontally. Mix butter, brown sugar, cinnamon, and pecans in a small bowl.

Place 4 biscuit halves along the bottom of a lightly greased loaf pan. Drizzle with one-third of the butter mixture. Repeat another two layers. Top with remaining 4 biscuits. Bake for 20–30 minutes or until golden brown. Makes 8 servings.

# CINNAMON BISCUIT FANS

|                    |                        |
|-------------------:|:-----------------------|
| 1 can (16.3 ounces) | **flaky biscuits**     |
| 3 tablespoons      | **sugar**              |
| 1 teaspoon         | **cinnamon**           |
| 3 tablespoons      | **butter,** melted     |

Icing:

|                    |                        |
|-------------------:|:-----------------------|
| ½ cup              | **powdered sugar**     |
| ¼ tablespoon       | **vanilla**            |
| 3 teaspoons        | **milk**               |

Preheat oven to 400 degrees.

Cut each biscuit in half horizontally. In a small bowl, mix sugar and cinnamon. Coat each biscuit half with butter and sprinkle with sugar mixture. Cut each half into 5 strips.

Lightly grease 8 muffin cups. Place 10 strips vertically in each cup so tips are sticking out. Bake 15–20 minutes or until golden brown. Remove from muffin cups.

In a medium bowl, combine powdered sugar, vanilla, and milk. Drizzle over warm biscuits. Makes 8 servings.

# CARAMEL APPLE PULL-APART BISCUITS

|  |  |
|---|---|
| 2 cans (12 ounces each) | **biscuits** |
| 1 cup | **brown sugar** |
| ½ cup | **whipping cream** |
| 1 teaspoon | **cinnamon** |
| 1 medium | **apple,** peeled and finely diced |

Preheat oven to 350 degrees.

Cut each biscuit into fourths and arrange evenly in a lightly greased bundt pan.

Combine brown sugar, cream, cinnamon, and apple. Pour over biscuits. Bake 30–35 minutes or until golden brown. Remove from oven and invert on serving plate. Leave pan over biscuits for at least 5 minutes. Makes 10–12 servings.

# PRALINE MELTAWAY BISCUITS

⅓ cup  **butter,** melted
⅓ cup  **brown sugar**
⅓ cup  **chopped pecans**
1 can (12 ounces)  **honey butter biscuits**

Preheat oven to 425 degrees.

Mix butter, brown sugar, and pecans in a medium bowl. Divide mixture evenly among 10 muffin cups. Top each with a biscuit. Bake 11–13 minutes or until golden brown. Remove from oven and invert pan onto baking sheet. Leave pan over biscuits for at least 5 minutes. Makes 10 servings.

# LEMON PULL-APART COFFEE CAKE

| | |
|---|---|
| ¼ cup | **sugar** |
| ⅓ cup | **chopped walnuts** |
| ¼ cup | **golden raisins** |
| 2 tablespoons | **butter,** melted |
| 1 teaspoon | **lemon juice** |
| 1 can (7 ounces) | **buttermilk biscuits** |

Icing:

| | |
|---|---|
| ½ cup | **powdered sugar** |
| 1 tablespoon | **lemon juice** |

Preheat oven to 400 degrees.

In a large bowl, combine sugar, walnuts, raisins, butter, and lemon juice.

Cut each biscuit into fourths. Toss pieces into sugar mixture. Place into a lightly greased 9-inch round baking pan. Bake 20–25 minutes or until golden brown. Immediately invert onto a wire rack.

Combine powdered sugar and lemon juice and drizzle over cake. Makes 8 servings.

# MAPLE BREAKFAST ROLLS

| | |
|---:|:---|
| ¼ cup | **butter,** melted |
| 1 cup | **brown sugar** |
| ½ cup | **chopped walnuts** |
| ⅓ cup | **maple syrup** |
| 1 package (8 ounces) | **cream cheese,** softened |
| ½ cup | **powdered sugar** |
| 2 cans (12 ounces each) | **biscuits** |

Preheat oven to 350 degrees.

In a medium bowl, combine butter, brown sugar, walnuts, and syrup. Spread into a greased 13 x 9-baking dish. In a mixing bowl, beat cream cheese and powdered sugar until smooth.

Flatten each biscuit into a 4-inch round. Spread a tablespoon of cream cheese down the center of each biscuit and fold over. Pinch to seal. Place, seam side down on sugar mixture. Bake for 25–30 minutes or until golden brown. Immediately invert on serving plate. Makes 10–15 servings.

# PINEAPPLE BISCUITS

|                      |                            |
|---------------------:|----------------------------|
| ½ cup                | **brown sugar**            |
| ¼ cup                | **butter,** melted         |
| I can (8 ounces)     | **crushed pineapple,** drained |
| ¾ teaspoon           | **cinnamon**               |
| I can (12 ounces)    | **biscuits**               |

Preheat oven to 425 degrees.

In a bowl, combine brown sugar, butter, pineapple, and cinnamon.
Spoon into 10 greased muffin cups. Place a biscuit in each cup. Bake
for 10–15 minutes or until golden brown. Let stand for 5 minutes.
Invert on baking sheet. Makes 10 servings.

# CINNAMON PULL-APART BREAD

|  |  |
|---:|:---|
| ¾ cup | **sugar** |
| 2 tablespoons | **cinnamon** |
| 2 cans (12 ounces each) | **biscuits** |
| ½ cup | **butter,** melted, divided |

Icing:

|  |  |
|---:|:---|
| 4 ounces | **cream cheese,** softened |
| ½ cup | **powdered sugar** |
| 1 tablespoon | **milk** |

Preheat oven to 350 degrees.

Mix sugar and cinnamon in medium bowl. Cut each biscuit into fourths. Roll in cinnamon sugar. Place half of the biscuit pieces in greased bundt pan. Drizzle with half of the butter. Top with remaining biscuit pieces, then drizzle with remaining butter. Sprinkle with remaining cinnamon sugar. Bake 30–35 minutes or until golden brown. Cool in pan 5 minutes. Invert onto serving plate.

Beat cream cheese and powdered sugar in small bowl with electric mixer on medium speed until well blended. Add milk and beat until well blended. Add additional milk until glaze is of desired consistency. Drizzle over warm bread. Makes 10 servings.

# MONKEY BREAD

| | |
|---:|:---|
| 1/2 cup | **sugar** |
| 1 teaspoon | **cinnamon** |
| 2 cans (12 ounces each) | **biscuits** |
| 1 1/4 cups | **brown sugar** |
| 1/2 cup | **butter or margarine** |

Preheat oven to 375 degrees.

Combine sugar and cinnamon in pie pan. Cut each biscuit into fourths and roll in cinnamon mixture. Place half of the biscuit pieces in a lightly greased bundt pan.

In small saucepan, combine butter and brown sugar. Stir over medium heat until combined and butter is melted. Bring to a boil. Remove from heat and pour half of the mixture over biscuits in bundt pan. Place remaining biscuit pieces in pan and top with remaining brown sugar mixture. Bake 30–35 minutes or until golden brown. Immediately invert on a serving plate and serve warm. Makes 8–12 servings.

# BREAKFAST

# BREAKFAST BISCUIT SANDWICHES

| | |
|---:|:---|
| 4 | **eggs** |
| 4 tablespoons | **milk** |
| ¼ teaspoon | **salt** |
| ¼ teaspoon | **pepper** |
| 2 tablespoons | **grated sharp cheddar cheese** |
| I can (16.3 ounces) | **buttermilk biscuits** |
| 8 slices | **bacon,** cooked |

Preheat oven to 375 degrees.

Place biscuits on baking sheet and lightly grease 8 muffin cups.

In small bowl, mix eggs, milk, salt, pepper, and cheese and then pour evenly into muffin cups. Place biscuits and eggs in oven. Bake for 15–17 minutes or until biscuits are golden brown and eggs are fully cooked.

Cut warm biscuits in half horizontally. Place eggs and bacon on bottom halves of biscuits. Cover with top halves of biscuits. Makes 8 servings.

# CHEDDAR BISCUIT QUICHE

| | |
|---:|:---|
| I can (7 ounces) | **flaky biscuits** |
| 2 cups | **grated cheddar cheese** |
| 2 tablespoons | **flour** |
| 3 | **eggs,** slightly beaten |
| I ¼ | **cups milk** |
| ¾ cup | **chopped ham** |
| ¼ | **cup diced tomato** |
| I can (3 ounces) | **diced mild green chile** |
| ½ teaspoon | **salt** |
| ¼ teaspoon | **pepper** |

Preheat oven to 350 degrees.

Line the bottom and the sides of 9-inch pie pan with biscuits and press together to seal. Combine cheese and flour. Add eggs, milk, ham, tomato, chile, salt, and pepper. Mix well and then pour into pan. Bake for 50–55 minutes. Makes 8 servings.

# SAUSAGE QUICHE

| | |
|---:|:---|
| 1 pound | **breakfast sausage** |
| 1/4 cup | **chopped onion** |
| 1/4 cup | **chopped green bell pepper** |
| 10 | **eggs** |
| 1 cup | **grated cheddar cheese** |
| 1 can (16.3 ounces) | **biscuits** |

Preheat oven to 375 degrees.

In a large frying pan, brown sausage with onion and bell pepper. Drain well. In a large bowl, beat eggs and then stir in cheese and sausage. Line the bottom and the sides of a lightly greased 13 x 9-inch baking dish with biscuits and press together to seal. Pour egg mixture into dish. Bake for 30–35 minutes or until eggs have set and crust is golden brown. Makes 8 servings.

# HERBED BISCUIT EGG BAKE

| | |
|---:|:---|
| I can (7 ounces) | **biscuits** |
| I | **onion,** chopped |
| I tablespoon | **butter** |
| 7 | **eggs** |
| I teaspoon | **garlic powder** |
| ½ teaspoon | **dried tarragon** |
| ½ teaspoon | **dried thyme** |
| ½ teaspoon | **lemon pepper** |
| ½ teaspoon | **salt** |
| 2 cups | **chopped broccoli,** steamed |
| I cup | **grated cheddar cheese** |

Preheat oven to 400 degrees.

Line the bottom and the sides of a lightly greased 8 x 8-inch baking pan with biscuits and press together to seal. In a frying pan, saute onions in butter. Spread evenly on biscuits.

In a bowl, mix eggs and spices and then pour into crust. Add broccoli and sprinkle top with cheese. Bake for 35–40 minutes or until eggs are set and crust is golden brown. Makes 4 servings.

# BACON QUICHE TARTS

| | |
|---:|:---|
| I can (12 ounces) | **biscuits** |
| I package (8 ounces) | **cream cheese,** softened |
| 2 tablespoons | **milk** |
| 2 | **eggs** |
| ½ cup | **grated Swiss cheese** |
| 5 slices | **bacon,** cooked and crumbled |
| I tablespoon | **dried onion flakes** |

Preheat oven to 375 degrees.

Press each biscuit firmly in the bottom and up the sides of a lightly greased muffin cup.

In a medium bowl combine cream cheese, milk, and eggs; beat until smooth. Stir in cheese, bacon, and onion flakes and then spoon evenly into each muffin cup. Bake 20–25 minutes until eggs have set and the biscuits are golden brown. Makes 10 servings.

# SCRAMBLED EGGS ALFREDO BAKE

| | |
|---|---|
| 2 tablespoons | **butter** |
| 1/4 cup | **chopped onion** |
| 1/4 cup | **chopped green bell pepper** |
| 1 jar (4.5 ounces) | **sliced mushrooms** |
| 12 | **eggs,** beaten |
| 1/3 cup | **cooked and crumbled bacon** |
| 3/4 cup | **Alfredo sauce** |
| 1 can (7 ounces) | **biscuits** |

Preheat oven to 400 degrees.

Melt butter in a frying pan over medium heat. Saute onion, bell pepper, and mushrooms, stirring occasionally, until vegetables are tender. Add eggs. Cook, stirring occasionally, until eggs are set; remove from heat. Gently stir in bacon and Alfredo sauce. Spread into a lightly greased 8 x 8-inch baking dish. Top with biscuits. Bake uncovered about 15 minutes until biscuits are golden brown. Makes 6 servings.

# ROASTED VEGETABLE STRATA

| | |
|---:|:---|
| 1 can (16.3 ounces) | **buttermilk biscuits** |
| 4 | **eggs** |
| 3 cups | **milk** |
| 2 tablespoons | **olive oil** |
| 1 teaspoon | **pepper** |
| 8 medium | **green onions,** sliced |
| 2 cups | **grated Monterey Jack cheese** |
| 5 small | **mushrooms,** sliced |
| 1 | **red bell pepper,** diced |
| 1 | **yellow bell pepper,** diced |
| 1 | **small zucchini,** thinly sliced |

Bake biscuits according to package directions. Then preheat oven to 450 degrees.

In large bowl, beat eggs, milk, oil, and pepper until blended. Break biscuits into random-sized pieces; spread in ungreased 13 x 9-inch glass baking dish. Pour egg mixture over biscuits. Sprinkle with onions and cheese. Cover; refrigerate at least 8 hours but no longer than 24 hours.

In a lightly greased 15 x 10-inch or 13 x 9-inch pan, stir together vegetables. Bake 15–20 minutes, stirring occasionally, until vegetables are tender. Cover and refrigerate.

When ready to bake, preheat oven to 350 degrees. Stir biscuit mixture in dish. Top with vegetables. Cover with foil and bake for 30 minutes; uncover and bake an additional 20–25 minutes or until top is golden brown and knife inserted in center comes out clean. Serve warm. Makes 12–15 servings.

# BREAKFAST POCKETS

|              |                                                 |
|-------------:|:------------------------------------------------|
| ¼ cup | **chopped onion** |
| 1 ¼ cups | **grated hash browns** |
| 4 | **eggs,** beaten |
| 1 ½ tablespoons | **milk** |
| ¼ teaspoon | **salt** |
| ¼ teaspoon | **pepper** |
| ¼ teaspoon | **garlic salt** |
| dash | **hot sauce** |
| ½ pound | **sausage or bacon,** cooked, drained and crumbled |
| 1 ½ cups | **grated cheddar cheese** |
| 1 can (16.3 ounces) | **biscuits** |

Preheat oven to 350 degrees.

In a frying pan combine onions, hash browns, eggs, milk, and seasonings. Cook, stirring regularly until eggs have set. Stir in meat. Sprinkle in cheese and mix.

Flatten biscuits into 6-inch rounds. Top each with about ⅓ cup egg mixture. Fold dough over and pinch edges to seal. Bake for 15–20 minutes or until golden brown. Makes 8 servings.

# HAM AND CHEESE CASSEROLE

| | |
|---:|:---|
| I can (16.3 ounces) | **biscuits** |
| 3 cups | **grated cheddar cheese** |
| 2 cups | **diced ham** |
| 4 tablespoons | **diced onion** |
| 6 | **eggs** |
| I $\frac{1}{2}$ | **cups milk** |
| dash | **salt** |
| $\frac{1}{4}$ | **teaspoon pepper** |

Preheat oven to 425 degrees.

Line the bottom of a lightly greased 9 x 13-inch baking dish with biscuits and press together to form a crust. Sprinkle cheese evenly across biscuits. Top with ham and sprinkle with onion.

Mix eggs, milk, salt, and pepper together. Pour over onion layer. Bake for 20–25 minutes or until knife inserted in center comes out clean. Let set a few minutes before serving. Makes 8 servings.

# BREAKFAST SANDWICHES

I can (16.3 ounces) **biscuits**  
8 **sausage patties,** cooked  
8 slices **American cheese**

Bake biscuits according to package directions. Brown sausage patties. Cut biscuits in half and place sausage patty on bottom half. Top with a slice of American cheese and replace top. Makes 8 servings.

# HAM AND EGG PIZZAS

|  |  |
|---:|:---|
| 3 | **red, green, or yellow bell peppers,** cut into thin strips |
| 1 | **onion,** sliced |
| 1 ½ teaspoons | **unsalted butter** |
| 2 cups | **diced ham** |
| 1 can (12 ounces) | **biscuits** |
| 3 cups | **grated Monterey Jack cheese** |
| 10 | **eggs** |

Preheat oven to 425 degrees.

In a large frying pan, saute bell peppers and onions in butter. Stir in ham and remove from heat.

Flatten each biscuit into a 6-inch round. Divide the cheese among the biscuits and top it with the bell pepper mixture, making a well in the center. Crack and drop an egg carefully into the well of each shell. Bake the pizzas for 12–15 minutes, or until the egg yolks are set. Makes 10 servings.

# SAUSAGE BISCUIT PINWHEELS

| | |
|---:|:---|
| 1 can (12 ounces) | **flaky biscuits** |
| 8 ounces | **ground sausage** |
| 2 tablespoons | **onion flakes** |

Flatten each biscuit into a 5-inch round. Place biscuits in two rows of five. Pinch edges together and roll out to form one large rectangle. Spread raw sausage evenly across dough and sprinkle onion flakes on top. Roll dough lengthwise to form one long log. Wrap in wax paper and refrigerate for at least one hour to firm dough.

Preheat oven to 350 degrees. Unwrap log and slice into 24 pinwheels. Place on a lightly greased baking sheet and bake for 20–25 minutes. Makes 24 servings.

# BEAR CLAWS

| | |
|---:|:---|
| 4 ounces | **cream cheese,** softened |
| ¼ cup | **orange marmalade** |
| I can (12 ounces) | **flaky biscuits** |
| ¼ cup | **sliced almonds** |
| I tablespoon | **sugar** |
| ¼ cup | **orange juice** |

Preheat oven to 375 degrees.

Combine cream cheese and marmalade in a bowl. Blend well.

Cut biscuit in half horizontally. Flatten into 4-inch rounds. Spoon
I tablespoon cream cheese mixture into the center of 10 biscuits.
Moisten edges and place another biscuit on top. Press firmly around
edges with a fork to seal. With a knife cut five ¼-inch slits, I inch apart
around one side of the biscuit to resemble a bear claw.

In a small bowl, combine almonds and sugar. Brush top of each biscuit
with orange juice. Sprinkle with almond mixture. Place biscuits on a
baking sheet. Bake for 15–20 minutes or until golden brown. Makes 10
servings.

# APPLE COFFEE CAKE

|  |  |
|---:|:---|
| 2 | **apples,** cored, peeled and chopped, divided |
| I can (12 ounces) | **flaky biscuits** |
| I tablespoon | **butter,** softened |
| 1/3 cup | **brown sugar** |
| 1/2 teaspoon | **cinnamon** |
| 1/3 cup | **light corn syrup** |
| I 1/2 | **teaspoons vanilla** |
| I | **egg** |
| 1/2 cup | **chopped pecans** |

Icing:

|  |  |
|---:|:---|
| 1/3 cup | **powdered sugar** |
| 1/4 teaspoon | **vanilla** |
| I tablespoon | **milk** |

Preheat oven to 350 degrees.

Place two-thirds of apple pieces in a lightly greased 9-inch baking dish. Cut each biscuit into fourths. Arrange biscuit triangles in dish resting on their circular edge with the points up. Top with remaining apples.

Combine butter, brown sugar, cinnamon, corn syrup, vanilla, and egg. Beat for 2–3 minutes or until sugar is partially dissolved. Stir in pecans and then spoon over biscuits. Bake for 35–45 minutes or until golden brown. Combine powdered sugar, vanilla, and milk and then drizzle over warm cake. Makes 8 servings.

# DOUGHNUTS

|            |                              |
|-----------:|:-----------------------------|
| I can (12 ounces) | **honey butter biscuits** |
| I cup | **powdered sugar** |
|  | **oil,** for frying |

Preheat oil to 350 degrees.

Flatten biscuits slightly. Punch a whole in the center of each biscuit. Place biscuit in fryer for 30 seconds on each side. Dip in powdered sugar. Makes 10 servings.

# BLUEBERRY MONKEY BREAD

|  |  |
|---|---|
| ⅔ cup | **sugar** |
| 2 tablespoons | **cinnamon,** divided |
| 2 cans (16.3 ounces each) | **buttermilk biscuits** |
| 1 ¼ cups | **blueberries,** divided |
| ⅔ cup | **brown sugar** |
| 8 tablespoons | **butter** |
| 1 teaspoon | **vanilla** |

Preheat oven to 350 degrees. Thoroughly grease a bundt pan.

Mix sugar and 1 tablespoon cinnamon. Cut each biscuit into fourths. Roll each piece in sugar mixture. Place biscuits in a large bowl, add ¼ cup blueberries and toss gently to evenly distribute berries. Put mixture in pan.

In saucepan, combine brown sugar, butter, vanilla, remaining cinnamon, and the remaining blueberries. Bring to a boil and then reduce heat to low. Cook, stirring frequently, until sugar is dissolved and margarine melted. Pour over biscuits. Bake for 30–35 minutes or until done. Place serving plate, face down, on pan and then invert; remove pan. Makes 8–10 servings.

LUNCH

# BEEFY PEPPER BISCUITS

|  |  |
|---|---|
| I can (16.3 ounces) | **biscuits** |
| I can (10 ounces) | **French onion soup,** condensed |
| 10 ounces | **deli sliced beef,** cut into strips |
| I large | **green bell pepper,** chopped |
| ½ teaspoon | **garlic pepper blend** |
| I ⅓ cups | **water,** divided |
| ⅓ cup | **flour** |

Bake biscuits according to package directions.

In a 2-quart saucepan, mix soup, beef, bell peppers, garlic pepper, and I cup water. Heat to boiling over medium-high heat and then reduce to medium-low. In a small bowl, stir remaining water and flour until mixed; stir into beef mixture. Heat to boiling, stirring frequently until thickened. Serve warm over halved biscuits. Makes 8 servings.

# BROCCOLI AND TUNA ON BISCUITS

| | |
|---|---|
| 1 can (16.3 ounces) | **biscuits** |
| 2 cups | **frozen chopped broccoli** |
| 2 cups | **milk** |
| 1/4 cup | **Bisquick mix** |
| 1/4 cup | **grated Parmesan cheese** |
| 1 can (12 ounces) | **chunk tuna,** drained |
| 1/8 teaspoon | **pepper** |

Bake biscuits and cook broccoli according to package directions.

In a 2-quart saucepan, stir milk and Bisquick with a metal whisk until completely smooth. Cook over medium heat 9–11 minutes, stirring constantly, until sauce thickens. Gently stir in cheese, tuna, and pepper. Cook 1–3 minutes, stirring constantly until hot. Cut biscuits in half and cover the halves with tuna mixture and then top with broccoli. Makes 8 servings.

# BARBECUE PORK SANDWICHES

|  |  |
|---|---|
| 2 cans (16.3 ounces each) | **biscuits** |
| 2 containers (18 ounces each) | **refrigerated barbeque shredded pork** |
| 2 cups | **frozen mixed vegetables,** thawed and drained |
| 4 tablespoons | **maple syrup** |

Bake biscuits according to package directions.

Place pork in a microwavable bowl. Cover with microwavable plastic wrap, folding one edge back $\frac{1}{4}$ inch to vent steam. Microwave on high for 2 minutes; stir. Repeat if pork is not hot enough. Stir in vegetables and maple syrup. Cover and microwave on high for 1 minute. Cut biscuits in half and top each half with barbeque pork. Makes 16 servings.

# CHEDDAR BISCUITS WITH HAM SALAD

|  |  |
|---:|:---|
| ½ cup | **grated sharp cheddar cheese** |
| I can (16.3 ounces) | **buttermilk biscuits** |
| 2 | **green onions,** chopped |
| I small | **celery rib,** cut into small pieces |
| I | **jalapeno,** seeded and quartered |
| ½ pound | **sliced smoked ham,** chopped |
| ¼ cup | **mayonnaise** |
| I tablespoon | **Dijon mustard** |
|  | **salt and pepper to taste** |

Spread cheese evenly on a flat surface. Lightly press biscuit tops into cheese and place on a baking sheet, cheese side up. Bake according to package directions.

In a food processor, pulse onions, celery, and jalapeno until finely chopped. Add ham and pulse just until finely chopped. Pulse in mayonnaise and mustard; season lightly with salt and pepper. Cut biscuits in half; place salad between halves and serve. Makes 8 servings.

# BUTTERMILK BISCUITS WITH TOMATO GRAVY

| | |
|---:|:---|
| I can (16.3 ounces) | **buttermilk biscuits** |
| 3 large | **tomatoes** |
| ½ cup | **butter or margarine** |
| ½ cup | **self-rising flour** |
| 2 ½ cups | **water** |
| ½ cup | **milk** |
| | **salt and pepper,** to taste |
| ¼ cup | **grated mozzarella cheese** |
| ¼ cup | **grated cheddar cheese** |

Bake biscuits according to package directions.

Peel and dice tomatoes into a bowl, reserving the juice. In a saucepan, melt butter; add flour and stir until browned. Gradually add water and then stir in tomatoes and juice. Add milk, salt, and pepper; simmer for 15 minutes. Serve over halved biscuits. Top with cheeses. Makes 8 servings.

# TOMATO AND KIELBASA SANDWICHES

| | |
|---|---|
| 1 can (16.3 ounces) | **biscuits** |
| 1/2 pound | **kielbasa,** cut into 1/2-inch slices |
| 1 pound | **plum tomatoes,** cut into 1/2-inch slices |
| 1/2 cup | **chopped onion** |
| 1 | **jalapeno,** seeded and minced* |
| 1/3 cup | **chopped cilantro** |
| 1 1/2 tablespoons | **lime juice** |
| | **salt,** to taste |
| 2/3 cup | **sour cream** |
| 2 teaspoons | **water** |

Bake biscuits according to package directions.

Brown kielbasa in a large frying pan over medium heat. Transfer to a bowl. In same frying pan, saute tomatoes, onion, and jalapeno, stirring until the tomatoes are softened. Add tomato mixture to sausage and toss with cilantro, lime juice, and salt to taste.

Mix sour cream with water. Cut biscuits in half. Top each half with kielbasa mixture and sour cream. Makes 16 servings.

*Reduce the amount of jalapeno for a less spicy sandwich.

# CALZONES

| | |
|---:|:---|
| ½ pound | **Italian pork sausage** |
| ⅓ cup | **chopped onion** |
| ¼ cup | **chopped red bell pepper** |
| 1 can (16.3 ounces) | **biscuits** |
| ½ cup | **grated mozzarella cheese** |
| 1 ½ cups | **marinara sauce,** warmed |

Preheat oven to 375 degrees.

In a medium frying pan brown sausage with onion and bell pepper over medium heat. Drain and let cool.

Flatten each biscuit into a 6-inch diameter. Top each round with sausage mixture and cheese. Fold dough over filling and press edges firmly with a fork to seal. Bake on an ungreased baking sheet for 12–15 minutes or until golden brown. Serve with marinara sauce for dipping. Makes 8 servings.

# TEX-MEX SANDWICHES

| | |
|---:|:---|
| ½ cup | **chopped roast beef** |
| ¼ cup | **taco sauce** |
| ¼ cup | **barbeque sauce** |
| ¼ cup | **sliced black olives** |
| ¼ cup | **sliced green olives** |
| ¼ cup | **sliced green onions** |
| ½ cup | **grated cheddar cheese** |
| 1 can (12 ounces) | **biscuits** |
| ½ cup | **sour cream** |
| 10 | **pimiento slices** |

Preheat oven to 350 degrees.

In a medium bowl combine beef, taco sauce, barbeque sauce, olives, onions, and cheese.

Flatten each biscuit into a 5-inch round. Place 5 biscuits on an ungreased baking sheet and top with beef mixture. Brush edges of biscuits with water and then place another biscuit on top and press edges together with a fork. Make an indentation in the top of the biscuit using a spoon. Bake for 14–22 minutes or until golden brown. Repeat indentation if necessary. Fill each indentation with a heaping teaspoon of sour cream. Garnish each with 2 pimiento slices. Makes 5 servings.

# MEATBALL BISCUITS

|  |  |
|--:|:--|
| 1 can (12 ounces) | **flaky biscuits** |
| 10 | **frozen,** cooked Italian-style meatballs, thawed and cut in half |
| 2 sticks | **string cheese,** each cut into 10 pieces |
| 2 tablespoons | **grated Parmesan cheese** |
| 1 teaspoon | **Italian seasoning** |
| 1/2 teaspoon | **garlic powder** |
| 1 cup | **pizza sauce,** warmed |

Preheat oven to 375 degrees.

Cut each biscuit in half horizontally. Flatten each half into a 3-inch round. Place one meatball half and one string cheese piece in center of round. Wrap dough around meatball and press edges to seal. Place seam side down on an ungreased baking sheet. Once all balls have been placed on sheet, sprinkle evenly with Parmesan cheese, Italian seasoning and garlic powder. Bake for 20–25 minutes or until golden brown and biscuits are no longer doughy in the center. Serve with pizza sauce for dipping. Makes 20 servings.

# SAMMICHES

| | |
|---:|:---|
| 1 can (12 ounces) | **biscuits** |
| 10 slices | **lunch meat (turkey,** ham, or beef) |
| 10 slices | **American cheese** |
| 1 | **egg white** |

Preheat oven according to biscuit package directions.

Flatten each biscuit into a 5-inch round. Place a small amount of meat and a crumbled up piece of cheese on each round. Fold over and seal, use a fork to press edges if dough doesn't stick. Brush with egg white. Bake for 15 minutes or until golden. Makes 10 servings.

# MINI PIZZA BITES

|  |  |
|---:|:---|
| 1 can (16.3 ounces) | **biscuits** |
| 1 can (8 ounces) | **tomato sauce** |
| 1 cup | **grated sharp cheddar cheese** |
| 12 ounces | **ground beef,** cooked and drained |
| ½ cup | **minced green bell pepper** |
| ½ cup | **minced onion** |
| 4 ounces | **sliced pepperoni** |
| ½ cup | **grated mozzarella cheese** |

Preheat oven 425 degrees.

Cut each biscuit into 3 equal layers. Pinch up the edges of the circles to make a slight rim. Place on a greased baking sheet. Spread a little tomato sauce on each, top with rest of ingredients. Bake for 10–15 minutes or until crust is brown and toppings are bubbling. Makes 24 pieces.

# HOT TURKEY SANDWICHES

|  |  |
|---|---|
| I can (16.3 ounces) | **biscuits** |
| I cup | **turkey gravy** |
| I pound | **thinly sliced turkey** |
| 2 cups | **moist stuffing** |

Prepare biscuits and turkey gravy according to package directions. Cut biscuits in half, top lower half with turkey, stuffing, and gravy. Replace top half. Serve warm. Makes 8 servings.

# BACON TOMATO BISCUIT MELTS

|  |  |
|---:|:---|
| 1 can (16.3 ounces) | **biscuits** |
| 3 large | **tomatoes,** sliced |
| 16 strips | **bacon,** cooked |
| 2 cups | **grated mozzarella cheese** |

Bake biscuits according to package directions. Set oven temperature to broil.

Divide the biscuits in half. Top each half with 1 slice of tomato and 1 slice of bacon and sprinkle with cheese. Broil on top rack 1–2 minutes or until cheese begins to brown. Makes 16 small open-faced sandwiches.

# SESAME HOT DOGS

|  |  |
|---:|:---|
| 8 | **hot dogs** |
| 8 slices | **American cheese** |
| 1 can (16.3 ounces) | **biscuits** |
| 2 tablespoons | **butter,** melted |
| ¼ cup | **sesame seeds** |

Preheat oven to 425 degrees.

Make a slit lengthwise in each hot dog. Fold a slice of cheese into fourths and place in the cut hot dog. Repeat for each hot dog. Flatten biscuits into 5-inch rounds. Wrap biscuits around each hot dog, brush with butter and sprinkle with sesame seeds. Place on a lightly greased baking sheet and bake for 1-1−13 minutes. Makes 8 servings.

# HAM BISCUIWICHES

|  |  |
|---:|:---|
| 1 can (16.3 ounces) | **biscuits** |
| 1/4 cup | **butter** |
| 1 tablespoon | **finely grated onion** |
| 1 1/2 tablespoons | **poppy seeds** |
| 1 teaspoon | **Dijon mustard** |
| 1 teaspoon | **Worcestershire sauce** |
| 10 | **thin slices baked ham** |
| 1 cup | **grated Swiss cheese** |

Bake biscuits according to package directions.

Beat butter, onion, poppy seeds, mustard, and Worcestershire sauce together. Split cooked biscuits in half and butter each side. Place on a lightly greased baking sheet. Place a slice of ham on the bottom half and sprinkle with cheese. Replace tops and cover with aluminum foil. Return biscuits to oven and bake until cheese has melted, about 5 minutes. Makes 8 servings.

# BARBECUPS

|  |  |
|---|---|
| 1 pound | **ground beef** |
| 1/2 cup | **barbecue sauce** |
| 1/4 cup | **chopped onion** |
| 2 tablespoons | **brown sugar** |
| 1 can (12 ounces) | **biscuits** |
| 1/2 cup | **grated cheddar cheese** |

Preheat oven to 400 degrees. Grease 10 muffin cups.

Brown ground beef in large frying pan, drain. Stir in barbeque sauce, onion, and brown sugar. Cook for a minute longer, stirring frequently.

Flatten each biscuit into a 4-inch round. Place a biscuit in each muffin cup, firmly pressing into the bottom and up the sides. Spoon beef mixture into muffin cups. Sprinkle with cheese. Bake for 10–12 minutes or until edges of biscuits are golden brown. Allow to cool before serving. Makes 10 servings.

# KRAUTBURGERS

|              |                          |
|-------------:|:-------------------------|
| 1 gallon | **water** |
| 1 head | **cabbage** |
| 4 pounds | **ground beef** |
| 4 large | **onions,** chopped |
| 1 tablespoon | **salt** |
| 2 tablespoons | **pepper** |
| 1 tablespoon | **garlic powder** |
| 2 cans (16.3 ounces each) | **flaky biscuits** |

Preheat oven to 375 degrees.

Fill a large pot with water and bring to a boil. Slice cabbage into thin strips. Place in water and boil until cabbage is limp, about 30 minutes. Drain.

In a frying pan, combine beef, onion, salt, pepper, and garlic powder. Cook over medium-high heat until meat is browned. Combine beef and cabbage and toss until evenly mixed.

Lightly grease two baking sheets. On a floured surface and with a floured rolling pin, roll biscuits until thin, about 7–8-inch squares. Place ½ cup mixture on each biscuit and pull up edges. Pinch dough to seal so no gaps are present and place pinched side down on baking sheet. Bake for 15–17 minutes or until golden brown. Makes 16 servings.

# CRAB SHORTCAKES

| | |
|---:|:---|
| 1 can (10 ounces) | **biscuits** |
| ½ cup | **white wine** |
| 1 jar (16 ounces) | **Alfredo sauce** |
| 1 package (8 ounces) | **cream cheese** |
| 1 cup | **frozen baby peas** |
| ½ pound | **shrimp,** shelled, deveined, and cooked |
| 1 can (6 ounces) | **crabmeat,** drained |
| ½ cup | **grated cheddar cheese** |
| ¼ cup | **sliced green onions** |

Bake biscuits according to package directions.

In large frying pan over high heat, cook wine for 3–5 minutes or until slightly reduced. Reduce heat to medium and add Alfredo sauce, cream cheese, peas, shrimp, and crabmeat; mix well. Simmer 8–10 minutes, stirring occasionally.

Cut biscuits in half and place bottom halves on individual serving plates. Spoon half of seafood mixture over biscuits. Cover with biscuit tops. Top with remaining seafood mixture. Sprinkle with cheese and onions. Makes 5 servings.

# CHICKEN CLUB BAKE

|  |  |
|---:|:---|
| 5 | **boneless, skinless chicken breasts,** uncooked |
| 5 tablespoons | **bacon bits** |
| 2 medium | **tomatoes,** sliced |
| 1 cup | **mayonnaise** |
| 1 cup | **grated mozzarella cheese** |
| 2 teaspoons | **basil** |
| 1 can (10 ounces) | **biscuits** |

Preheat oven to 375 degrees.

Place chicken breasts in a baking dish. Layer bacon bits on top of chicken. Next layer tomatoes.

In a medium bowl combine mayonnaise, cheese, and basil. Spread mixture over tomatoes. Place one biscuit on top of each chicken breast. Bake for 20 minutes or until biscuits are golden brown. Makes 5 servings.

DINNER

# ITALIAN CASSEROLE

|  |  |
|---|---|
| 1 pound | **ground beef** |
| ½ cup | **chopped onion** |
| ¾ cup | **water** |
| ¼ teaspoon | **pepper** |
| 1 can (8 ounces) | **tomato sauce** |
| 1 can (6 ounces) | **tomato paste** |
| 1 package (9 ounces) | **frozen mixed vegetables,** thawed |
| 2 cups | **grated mozzarella cheese,** divided |
| 1 can (12 ounces) | **buttermilk biscuits** |
| 1 tablespoon | **butter,** melted |
| ½ teaspoon | **oregano** |
| ¼ teaspoon | **basil** |

Preheat oven to 375 degrees.

In a large frying pan, brown beef and onion, and then drain. Stir in water, pepper, tomato sauce, and tomato paste. Simmer for 15 minutes, stirring occasionally. Remove from heat and stir in vegetables and 1-½ cup cheese. Spoon mixture into a 9 x 13-inch baking dish.

Cut each biscuit in half horizontally. Place biscuits along outer edges of dish, overlapping slightly. Sprinkle remaining cheese in center. Brush biscuits with butter and sprinkle with oregano and basil. Bake for 22–27 minutes or until biscuits are golden brown. Makes 6–8 servings.

# BISCUITS AND TUNA

| | |
|---:|:---|
| ½ cup | **chopped onion** |
| 2 tablespoons | **butter** |
| 6 tablespoons | **flour** |
| 2 teaspoons | **granulated chicken bouillon** |
| ¼ teaspoon | **salt** |
| ¼ teaspoon | **dried thyme** |
| ⅛ teaspoon | **pepper** |
| 2 cups | **milk** |
| 1 ½ cups | **water** |
| 1 can (13 ounces) | **canned tuna,** drained |
| 1 cup | **frozen peas,** thawed |
| 1 cup | **sliced carrots** |
| 3 tablespoons | **parsley** |
| 1 can (12 ounces) | **biscuits** |

Preheat oven to 400 degrees.

Saute onions in butter until tender. Stir in flour, bouillon, salt, thyme, and pepper. Add milk and water. Cook until thickened. Stir in tuna and vegetables. Heat until bubbly. Pour into a 9 x 13-inch baking dish. Separate biscuits and place on top. Bake for 12–15 minutes. Makes 6–8 servings.

# MEXICAN FIESTA BAKE

| | |
|---:|:---|
| 2 tablespoons | **butter,** melted |
| 1 can (16.3 ounces) | **buttermilk biscuits** |
| 1 can (10 ounces) | **buttermilk biscuits** |
| 1 jar (16 ounces) | **thick and chunky salsa** |
| 3 cups | **grated Monterey Jack cheese** |
| ½ cup | **chopped green bell pepper** |
| ½ cup | **sliced green onions** |
| 1 can (2.25 ounces) | **sliced black olives,** drained |

Preheat oven to 375 degrees.

Pour butter into a 13 x 9-inch baking dish and coat evenly.

Divide each biscuit into eight pieces, and then toss with salsa. Spoon evenly into baking dish. Sprinkle with cheese, bell pepper, onions and olives. Bake for 35–45 minutes or until edges are golden brown and center is baked. Makes 6–8 servings.

# TACO CASSEROLE

|                     |                                        |
|--------------------:|----------------------------------------|
| I can (12 ounces)   | **buttermilk biscuits**                |
| I jar (16 ounces)   | **medium taco sauce**                  |
| I ½ cups            | **grated sharp cheddar cheese,** divided |
| I ½ cups            | **grated mozzarella cheese,** divided  |
| ½ pound             | **ground beef**                        |
| ¼ cup               | **chopped green bell pepper**          |
| ¼ cup               | **chopped red bell pepper**            |
| I can (4 ounces)    | **mushrooms,** drained                 |
| I can (2.25 ounces) | **sliced black olives,** drained       |

Preheat oven to 400 degrees.

Cut each biscuit into fourths. In a large bowl toss biscuits in taco sauce. Place biscuits in a lightly greased 13 x 9-inch baking dish. Sprinkle with half the cheddar and mozzarella cheeses. Bake for 15–18 minutes or until bubbly and center is set.

In a large frying pan, brown ground beef with peppers and mushrooms and then drain. Sprinkle remaining cheeses and olives over biscuits and top with beef mixture. Bake an additional 5–7 minutes until mixture bubbles around edges. Makes 6–8 servings.

# SOUTHWESTERN BEAN BAKE

| | |
|---|---|
| I can (15 ounces) | **kidney beans,** drained and rinsed |
| I can (15 ounces) | **great northern beans,** drained and rinsed |
| I can (14.5 ounces) | **stewed tomatoes,** with juices |
| ½ cup | **salsa** |
| ¼ cup | **ketchup** |
| I can (12 ounces) | **buttermilk biscuits** |

Preheat oven to 375 degrees.

In a large saucepan, heat beans, tomatoes, salsa, and ketchup to boiling, stirring occasionally. Pour into a 9 x 13-inch baking dish.

Separate biscuits and place them evenly on top of bean mixture. Bake for 20–25 minutes or until biscuits are golden brown. Makes 6-8 servings

# TURKEY POT PIE

| | |
|---:|:---|
| 1 ½ cups | **cooked turkey** |
| 2 cups | **frozen peas and carrots** |
| 1 medium | **onion,** chopped |
| 1 jar (12 ounces) | **turkey gravy** |
| 1 can (12 ounces) | **buttermilk biscuits** |

Preheat oven to 375 degrees.

In a saucepan, heat turkey, vegetables, onion, and gravy to boiling; stirring frequently. Pour into a 9 x 9-inch baking dish. Separate biscuits, and then place biscuits evenly across the top of mixture. Bake for 20–25 minutes or until biscuits are golden brown. Makes 6–8 servings.

# CHICKEN AND BISCUIT CASSEROLE

|  |  |
|---:|:---|
| 2 cups | **cooked and cubed chicken** |
| 10 ounces | **broccoli,** steamed |
| 1 can (10.5 ounces) | **cream of chicken soup,** condensed |
| 1/4 cup | **chopped onion** |
| 1/4 cup | **sour cream** |
| 1 1/2 teaspoons | **Worcestershire sauce** |
| 1/2 cup | **grated cheddar cheese** |
| 1 can (7 ounces) | **flaky biscuits** |

Preheat oven to 375 degrees.

In a large bowl, combine chicken, broccoli, soup, onion, sour cream, and Worcestershire sauce. Pour into an 8 x 8-inch baking dish. Bake for 20–25 minutes or until bubbling.

Remove from oven and top with cheese. Arrange the biscuits across top of casserole and return to oven and bake an additional 25–30 minutes or until biscuits are golden brown. Makes 4 servings.

# BEEF POT PIE

|              |                              |
|-------------:|------------------------------|
| ½ pound      | **roast beef,** cubed        |
| 2 cups       | **frozen mixed vegetables**  |
| 1 medium     | **onion,** chopped           |
| 1 jar (12 ounces) | **beef gravy**          |
| 1 can (12 ounces) | **buttermilk biscuits** |

Preheat oven to 375 degrees.

In a large saucepan, combine beef, vegetables, onion, and gravy. Bring to a boil over medium heat, stirring regularly. Pour into a 9 x 9-inch baking dish. Separate biscuits, and then place them evenly across the top of mixture. Bake for 20–25 minutes or until biscuits are golden brown. Makes 4–6 servings.

# TURKEY AND BISCUITS

|  |  |
|---|---|
| ¼ cup | **butter,** melted |
| 2 cups | **cooked and cubed turkey** |
| ½ cup | **flour** |
| ½ teaspoon | **basil** |
| ¼ teaspoon | **salt** |
| ¼ teaspoon | **pepper** |
| I cup | **chicken broth** |
| ⅔ cup | **milk** |
| I | **red bell pepper,** cut into strips |
| I can (4 ounces) | **mushrooms,** drained |
| I cup | **fresh spinach,** cut into strips |
| I can (12 ounces) | **buttermilk biscuits** |

Preheat oven to 400 degrees.

In a large bowl, combine butter, turkey, flour, basil, salt, pepper, broth, milk, bell pepper, and mushrooms. Pour into a greased 9 x 9-inch baking dish. Bake 20 minutes, stirring once after 10 minutes.

Remove casserole from oven and stir in spinach. Separate biscuits, and then place them evenly on top of turkey mixture. Return to oven and continue to bake for 15–20 minutes longer until biscuits are golden brown. Makes 4–6 servings.

# PAN PIZZA

1 can (16.3 ounces) **biscuits**
1 can (14 ounces) **pizza sauce**
2 cups **grated mozzarella cheese,** divided
16 slices **pepperoni**

Preheat oven to 375 degrees.

Cut each biscuit into fourths. In a large bowl, combine biscuits, pizza sauce, and 1 cup cheese; toss to coat. Transfer mixture to an ungreased 9 x 9-inch baking dish. Top with pepperoni and the remaining cheese. Bake for 22–28 minutes or until golden brown and bubbly. Makes 4–6 servings.

# LOUISIANA SHRIMP CASSEROLE

| | |
|---:|:---|
| 2 tablespoons | **butter** |
| 1 teaspoon | **garlic,** minced |
| 1 | **red bell pepper,** cut into strips |
| 1 medium | **onion,** sliced |
| ¼ cup | **chopped celery** |
| 2 tablespoons | **Bisquick mix** |
| 1 can (14.5 ounces) | **diced tomatoes with juices** |
| ¼ teaspoon | **salt** |
| ¼ teaspoon | **Tabasco hot pepper sauce** |
| 12 ounces | **large shrimp,** peeled and deveined |
| 1 can (12 ounces) | **biscuits** |

Preheat oven to 400 degrees.

In a large frying pan over medium heat, melt butter and saute garlic, bell pepper, onion, and celery until vegetables are tender. Stir Bisquick into mixture until blended. Stir in tomatoes, salt, pepper sauce, and shrimp. Reduce heat to medium low and cook about 7 minutes, stirring occasionally, until thick and bubbling. Pour mixture into an ungreased 9 x 9-inch baking dish.

Separate biscuits, and then place them evenly over shrimp mixture. Bake 20–30 minutes or until biscuits are golden brown. Makes 4–6 servings.

# VEGETABLE CASSEROLE

|  |  |
|---:|:---|
| 1 medium | **onion,** chopped |
| 1 tablespoon | **butter** |
| 1 bag (16 ounces) | **frozen mixed vegetables** |
| 2 cups | **frozen chopped broccoli** |
| 1 jar (16 ounces) | **Alfredo sauce** |
| 1 can (12 ounces) | **biscuits** |

Preheat oven to 400 degrees.

In a large frying pan, saute onion in butter until tender. Add vegetables, broccoli, and Alfredo sauce. Cook over medium heat 5–6 minutes, stirring occasionally, until mixture comes to a light boil. Spoon into an ungreased 9 x 9-inch baking dish.

Separate biscuits, and then place them on top of mixture. Bake for 20–25 minutes until biscuits are golden brown. Makes 4–6 servings.

# HOT TURKEY SALAD

| | |
|---:|:---|
| ¼ cup | **mayonnaise** |
| 2 tablespoons | **Bisquick mix** |
| 2 cups | **cooked and cubed turkey** |
| ¼ cup | **grated cheddar cheese** |
| 2 | **celery stalks,** sliced |
| 2 | **green onions,** sliced |
| 1 can (7 ounces) | **buttermilk biscuits** |

Preheat oven to 425 degrees.

Combine mayonnaise and Bisquick and mix until well blended. Stir in turkey, cheese, celery, and onions. Separate biscuits and place around edges of a lightly greased 9 x 9-inch baking dish. Spoon turkey mixture into center. Bake for 18–20 minutes or until biscuits are golden brown and salad is hot. Makes 4–6 servings.

# SHRIMP NEWBURG

| | |
|---|---|
| 1 can (16.3 ounces) | **flaky biscuits** |
| 2 cans (10.5 ounces each) | **cream of shrimp soup,** condensed |
| ½ cup | **milk** |
| 2 cups | **small cooked shrimp** |
| ¾ cup | **frozen peas** |
| ¼ cup | **sherry** |
| 1 cup | **grated sharp cheddar cheese,** divided |

Bake biscuits according to package directions.

In medium pan over medium heat, stir together soup and milk until smooth. Add shrimp and peas. Bring to simmer and cook slowly for 5 minutes. Stir in sherry and half of the cheese. Separate biscuits on to individual plates, sprinkle with remaining cheese and spoon sauce over top. Makes 8 servings.

# BEEFY CHEESE BAKE

| | |
|---:|:---|
| 1 ½ pounds | **ground beef** |
| ½ cup | **chopped onion** |
| 1 package (8 ounces) | **cream cheese,** softened |
| 1/ 4 cup | **milk** |
| 1 can (10.5 ounces) | **cream of mushroom soup,** condensed |
| ⅓ cup | **sliced ripe olives,** optional |
| ¼ cup | **ketchup** |
| ½ teaspoon | **salt** |
| ¼ teaspoon | **pepper** |
| 1 can (7 ounces) | **biscuits** |

Preheat oven to 375 degrees.

Brown ground beef and onion in frying pan. In medium bowl, blend cream cheese and milk. Stir in soup, olives, ketchup, salt, and pepper. Combine with meat mixture in 2-quart casserole. Bake 30 minutes.

Arrange biscuits on top and bake 15–18 additional minutes or until biscuits are browned. Makes 6 servings.

# CHICKEN WITH BISCUIT STUFFING

|  |  |
|---:|:---|
| 4 | **boneless,** skinless chicken breasts |
| I can (10.5 ounces) | **cream of chicken soup,** condensed |
| I cup | **chopped celery** |
| I cup | **chopped onion** |
| ½ teaspoon | **salt** |
| ¼ teaspoon | **pepper** |
| I | **egg** |
| I can (7 ounces) | **biscuits** |

Preheat oven to 350 degrees.

Place chicken on bottom of a greased 13 x 9-inch baking pan.

In a large bowl, combine soup, celery, onion, salt, pepper, and egg. Mix until well blended. Cut each biscuit into 10 pieces and add to soup mixture, mixing well. Spoon evenly over chicken. Bake for 55–65 minutes. Makes 4 servings.

# DESSERTS

# MINI CHERRY PIES

|  |  |
| ---: | :--- |
| ¹/₂ cup | **flour** |
| ¹/₂ cup | **brown sugar** |
| 1 teaspoon | **cinnamon** |
| ¹/₂ cup | **butter,** softened |
| 1 can (16.3 ounces) | **flaky biscuits** |
| 1 can (2-1 ounces) | **cherry pie filling** |
| 1 cup | **whipped cream** |

Preheat oven to 375 degrees.

Combine flour, brown sugar, and cinnamon. Mix in butter until mixture is crumbly.

Cut each biscuit in half horizontally. Flatten into 5-inch rounds. Place into lightly greased muffin cups; press firmly into the bottom and up the sides. Fill cups evenly with pie filling. Top with sugar mixture. Bake 15–17 minutes or until biscuits are golden brown. Top with whipped cream. Makes 8 servings.

# FRUITY BISCUITS

| | |
|---:|:---|
| I can (14 ounces) | **fruit cocktail,** with liquid |
| 2 tablespoons | **flour** |
| I ¼ cups | **sugar,** divided |
| I can (16.3 ounces) | **biscuits** |
| 4 tablespoons | **butter,** melted |
| 2 teaspoons | **cinnamon** |

Preheat oven to 350 degrees.

In a saucepan, bring fruit cocktail to a boil then pour into an ungreased 13 x 9-inch baking dish.

Combine flour and ¾ cup sugar and then sprinkle evenly over fruit. Separate biscuits and place on top of fruit. Drizzle butter over top. Combine remaining sugar and cinnamon and then sprinkle evenly across biscuits. Bake for 20 minutes. Makes 10 servings.

# SWEET AND TANGY APRICOT BISCUITS

| | |
|---|---|
| 2 tablespoons | **sweetened powdered lemonade** |
| 2 tablespoons | **sugar** |
| 1 can (12 ounces) | **flaky biscuits** |
| 3 tablespoons | **butter,** melted |
| ½ cup | **miniature marshmallows** |
| ¼ cup | **apricot preserves** |
| 2 tablespoons | **chopped pecans** |

Preheat oven to 375 degrees. Grease a 9x9-inch baking pan.

Combine lemonade and sugar. Dip top of each biscuit in butter, then in sugar mixture. Place sugar side up in pan. Sprinkle remaining sugar over top. Make an indentation in each biscuit and fill with marshmallows. Combine preserves and nuts. Spoon over marshmallows. Bake for 17–20 minutes or until golden brown. Makes 10 servings.

# CRUNCHY PEANUT RING

| | |
|---:|:---|
| ½ cup | **butter** |
| 1 cup | **chopped peanuts** |
| ¾ cup | **brown sugar** |
| ¼ cup | **maple syrup** |
| 2 cans (12 ounces each) | **honey butter biscuits** |

Preheat oven to 350 degrees. Lightly grease a bundt pan.

Melt butter in a saucepan. Stir in peanuts, brown sugar, and maple syrup. Pour ¼ cup sugar mixture into pan. Separate biscuits and then stand each biscuit on end, slightly overlapping around the pan. Pour remaining sugar mixture over biscuits. Bake for 20–30 minutes or until golden brown. Let cool for 5 minutes and invert onto serving plate. Makes 8–10 servings.

# CHOCOLATE OATMEAL BARS

|  |  |
|---:|:---|
| I can (16.3 ounces) | **flaky biscuits** |
| I cup | **semisweet chocolate chips** |
| I can (14 ounces) | **sweetened condensed milk** |
| 2 cups | **oatmeal** |
| 1/3 cup | **brown sugar** |
| 1/2 cup | **butter,** melted |
| 2 teaspoons | **vanilla** |

Preheat oven to 400 degrees.

Cut each biscuit in half horizontally. Place biscuits in ungreased 13 x
9-inch baking pan. Press over bottom and up one inch on sides to form
a crust. Sprinkle chocolate chips over dough. Pour condensed milk over
chips. Combine remaining ingredients and spread evenly over top. Bake
15–20 minutes or until golden brown. Cool for 5 minutes and cut into
bars. Makes 3 dozen bars.

# PEACH PINWHEELS

|              |                      |
|-------------:|----------------------|
| ½ cup | **sugar** |
| 2 teaspoons | **vanilla** |
| 1 tablespoon | **flour** |
| 1 can (14 ounces) | **peaches,** drained |
| 2 teaspoons | **lemon juice** |
| ½ cup | **brown sugar** |
| 2 tablespoons | **ground ginger** |
| ½ teaspoon | **cinnamon** |
| 1 can (16.3 ounces) | **honey butter biscuits** |
| 1 tablespoon | **butter,** melted |
| 3 tablespoons | **powdered sugar** |

Preheat oven to 375 degrees.

Blend sugar, vanilla, and flour. Add peaches and lemon juice and toss. Pour mixture into 10-inch cake pan. Bake until bubbling, about 30 minutes.

Mix brown sugar, ginger, and cinnamon. Cut each biscuit in half horizontally. Brush center and sides of biscuits with melted butter. Top bottom half with sugar mixture. Replace top. Slice each biscuit into 4 strips. Twist strips and form into pinwheels.

Once peach mixture is bubbling, place pinwheels on top and return to oven. Bake until biscuits are golden brown, about 15 minutes. Cool for 10 minutes. Dust with powdered sugar and serve. Makes 10 servings.

# CHANTILLY CREAM STRAWBERRY SHORTCAKE

| | |
|---:|:---|
| I can (16.3 ounces) | **biscuits** |
| 4 pints | **strawberries,** quartered |
| ½ cup | **Grand Mariner** |
| ½ cup | **sugar** |
| 2 tablespoons | **lemon juice** |
| I cup | **heavy cream** |
| 2 tablespoons | **powdered sugar** |

Bake biscuits according to package directions.

In a mixing bowl, combine strawberries, Grand Mariner, sugar, and lemon juice. Stir gently. Let stand at room temperature until juices form.

In a chilled mixing bowl, whisk cream until it begins to thicken. Add powdered sugar and continue to whisk until peaks form.

Cut biscuits in half horizontally and place bottom halves in a bowl or on a plate. Spoon strawberries evenly among biscuits. Top with cream and biscuit top. Drizzle remaining juice from strawberries evenly among biscuits. Makes 8 servings.

# APPLE UPSIDE-DOWN CAKE

| | |
|---:|:---|
| 3 tablespoons | **unsalted butter** |
| ½ cup | **brown sugar** |
| 1 pound | **apples,** peeled, cored and cut into thin wedges |
| 1 can (12 ounces) | **honey butter biscuits** |

Preheat oven to 400 degrees.

Heat butter over moderate heat until foam disappears. Stir in brown sugar and remove from heat. Spread evenly along bottom of well-greased 9-inch pie pan. Place apples, slightly overlapping, evenly around pan. Top with biscuits. Bake for 15–20 minutes or until biscuits are golden. Cool about 3 minutes. Invert cake onto serving plate. Makes 10 servings.

# ORANGE BISCUITS

| | |
|---:|:---|
| 1 can (16.3 ounces) | **biscuits** |
| ¼ cup | **sugar** |
| 1 teaspoon | **cinnamon** |
| 1 cup | **orange juice,** divided |
| ½ cup | **sugar** |
| 3 tablespoons | **butter,** melted |
| 2 teaspoons | **grated orange peel** |

Preheat oven to 400 degrees.

Cut each biscuit into fourths. Combine ¼ cup sugar and cinnamon in a small bowl. Dip each biscuit piece in ½ cup orange juice and coat with sugar mixture. Place in a lightly greased 9-inch baking pan.

Combine ½ cup sugar, ½ cup orange juice, melted butter, and orange peel. Pour over biscuits. Bake 20–25 minutes. Makes 10 servings.

# MARMALADE BISCUITS

|              |                            |
|-------------:|----------------------------|
| 1 cup | **orange marmalade** |
| 4 tablespoons | **butter,** softened |
| 1 can (12 ounces) | **honey butter biscuits** |

Preheat oven to 425 degrees.

Combine butter and marmalade, mixing well. Coat bottom of an 8-inch baking dish with mixture. Separate biscuits and place evenly in pan. Bake for 15–20 minutes or until biscuits are golden. Immediately invert onto a serving plate. Makes 10 servings.

# WHITE CHOCOLATE BERRY BREAD PUDDING

| | |
|---|---|
| I can (12 ounces) | **honey butter biscuits** |
| 3/4 cup | **grated white chocolate baking bars** |
| 2/3 cups | **sugar** |
| 3 1/2 cups | **milk** |
| 1 1/2 cups | **whipping cream** |
| 2 tablespoons | **butter,** melted |
| I tablespoon | **vanilla** |
| 4 | **eggs** |
| I cup | **raspberries,** frozen |
| I cup | **blueberries,** frozen |

Sauce:

| | |
|---|---|
| 1/3 cup | **sugar** |
| 2 tablespoons | **Bisquick mix** |
| I cup | **raspberries,** frozen |
| I cup | **blueberries,** frozen |
| 1/2 cup | **water** |

Bake biscuits according to package directions. Break up biscuits into pieces; spread in a 13 x 9-inch baking dish. Sprinkle with white chocolate. In large bowl, beat sugar, milk, whipping cream, butter, vanilla, and eggs with electric mixer on low speed until blended. Pour over biscuits in baking dish. Cover and refrigerate at least 8 hours but no longer than 24 hours.

Preheat oven to 350 degrees. Stir berries into biscuit mixture. Bake uncovered about I hour or until golden brown and toothpick inserted in center comes out clean.

In a saucepan, combine sugar and Bisquick mix. Stir in berries, and water. Cook over medium heat, stirring constantly, until mixture thickens and boils. Boil and stir I minute; remove from heat. Serve pudding warm topped with sauce and fresh berries. Store in refrigerator. Makes 10 servings.

# CARAMEL BISCUIT BITES

|              |                    |
|-------------:|:-------------------|
| 1 can (16.3 ounces) | **biscuits** |
| 1 teaspoon | **sugar** |
| 1/8 teaspoon | **cinnamon** |
| 2 tablespoons | **caramel apple dip** |
| 2 teaspoons | **milk** |
| 1 teaspoon | **chopped pecans** |

Bake biscuits according to package directions.

In serving bowl, mix sugar and cinnamon. Cut each biscuit into 8 wedges; toss them in the sugar mixture.

In small microwavable bowl, mix caramel apple dip, and milk. Microwave uncovered on high 15–30 seconds or until melted and hot. Evenly distribute biscuit pieces in eight dessert bowls. Stir caramel and drizzle over biscuit pieces. Sprinkle with pecans. Makes 8 servings.

# SWEET POTATO BREAD PUDDING

| | |
|---:|:---|
| 1 can (16.3 ounces) | **biscuits** |
| 1 cup | **chopped pecans** |
| ½ cup | **raisins** |
| 2½ cups | **milk** |
| 2½ cups | **half-and-half** |
| 1¼ cups | **mashed,** baked sweet potatoes |
| 1 cup | **sugar** |
| ¼ cup | **butter,** melted |
| 1 tablespoon | **vanilla** |
| ½ teaspoon | **cinnamon** |
| ½ teaspoon | **nutmeg** |
| 4 | **eggs** |

Sauce:

| | |
|---:|:---|
| 2 cups | **powdered sugar** |
| 1 cup | **butter,** melted |
| ½ cup | **orange juice** |
| 2 teaspoons | **cornstarch** |
| 4 | **egg yolks,** beaten |

Bake biscuits according to package directions. Break biscuits into random-sized pieces. Butter bottom and sides of a 13 x 9-inch baking pan. Spread biscuit pieces in pan. Sprinkle with pecans and raisins. In large bowl, beat all remaining pudding ingredients with electric mixer on low speed until blended. Pour over biscuits. Cover and refrigerate at least 2 hours but no longer than 8 hours.

Preheat oven to 350 degrees. Stir mixture in pan. Bake 1 hour or until top is golden and toothpick inserted in center comes out clean.

Meanwhile, in saucepan, heat all sauce ingredients over low heat 5–10 minutes, stirring constantly with wire whisk, until slightly thickened and temperature reaches 165 degrees for 15 seconds. Serve warm over pudding. Store covered in refrigerator. Makes 10 servings.

# BISCUIT COOKIES

|                        |                   |
| ---------------------- | ----------------- |
| 1 can (16.3 ounces)    | **biscuits**      |
| ½ cup                  | **chocolate chips** |
| ½ cup                  | **brown sugar**   |
| 2 teaspoons            | **margarine**     |

Preheat oven to 325 degrees.

Cut each biscuit in half horizontally. Flatten into 4-inch rounds. Cut into fourths or cut into shapes with a cookie cutter. Place on a lightly greased baking sheet.

Mix chocolate chips, sugar, and margarine in a microwave safe bowl. Cook in microwave for about 2 minutes on high until chocolate has completely melted. Stir well. Spread chocolate mixture over biscuits. Bake for 8–10 minutes. Makes approximately 32 cookies.

# DOUGHNUT PARFAIT

| | |
|---:|:---|
| I can (7 ounces) | **biscuits** |
| | **oil,** for frying |
| ½ cup | **powdered sugar** |
| 2 cups | **cold milk** |
| I box (3.4 ounces) | **instant vanilla pudding mix** |
| I to 2 medium | **firm bananas,** sliced |
| 2 cups | **whipped cream** |

In a large frying pan or fryer, preheat oil to 350 degrees. Cut each biscuit into fourths. Place in oil for 30 seconds or until golden brown. Remove and toss in powdered sugar. Set aside to cool.

In a bowl, whisk milk and pudding for 2 minutes. Let stand for 2 minutes or until pudding has set. Place four doughnuts in each of four parfait glasses. Top with pudding, bananas, and whipped cream. Repeat layers. Makes 4 servings.

# APPLE TURNOVERS

| | |
|---|---|
| I can (16.3 ounces) | **biscuits** |
| I can (14 ounces) | **apple pie filling** |
| I tablespoon | **cinnamon** |
| 4 tablespoons | **sugar** |

Preheat oven to 400 degrees.

Flatten each biscuit into a 6-inch round. Place 2 heaping tablespoons of pie filling on each biscuit. Moisten edges of dough with water. Fold over and press edges firmly with a fork to seal. Place on a lightly greased baking sheet.

Mix cinnamon and sugar and then sprinkle over top of biscuits. Bake for 15–20 minutes or until golden brown. Makes 8 servings.

# FRIED FRUIT PIES

|           |                        |
|-----------|------------------------|
| 3 cups | **mixed dried fruit** |
| I can (7 ounces) | **honey butter biscuits** |
|           | **oil,** for frying |
|           | **sugar** |

Place dried fruit in pot and cover with cold water. Bring to a boil, reduce heat and cook until tender and sweeten to taste.

Flatten each biscuit into a 4-inch round. Evenly distribute fruit among biscuits,  fold over and press edges firmly with a fork to seal. Fry in hot oil for 30 seconds  on each side. Sprinkle with sugar. Makes 10 servings.

# NOTES

# NOTES

# NOTES

# NOTES

# NOTES

# NOTES

# METRIC CONVERSION CHART

**Volume Measurements**

| U.S. | Metric |
| --- | --- |
| 1 teaspoon | 5 ml |
| 1 tablespoon | 15 ml |
| 1/4 cup | 60 ml |
| 1/3 cup | 75 ml |
| 1/2 cup | 125 ml |
| 2/3 cup | 150 ml |
| 3/4 cup | 175 ml |
| 1 cup | 250 ml |

**Weight Measurements**

| U.S. | Metric |
| --- | --- |
| 1/2 ounce | 15 g |
| 1 ounce | 30 g |
| 3 ounces | 90 g |
| 4 ounces | 115 g |
| 8 ounces | 225 g |
| 12 ounces | 350 g |
| 1 pound | 450 g |
| 2 1/4 pounds | 1 kg |

**Temperature Conversion**

| Fahrenheit | Celsius |
| --- | --- |
| 250 | 120 |
| 300 | 150 |
| 325 | 160 |
| 350 | 180 |
| 375 | 190 |
| 400 | 200 |
| 425 | 220 |
| 450 | 230 |

Check out these "101" favorites
for more tasty recipes:

| | |
|---|---|
| **Bacon** | **More Ramen** |
| **BBQ** | **More Slow Cooker** |
| **Beans** | **Peanut Butter** |
| **Beer** | **Pumpkin** |
| **Cake Mix** | **Ramen Noodles** |
| **Casserole** | **Rice** |
| **Chile Peppers** | **Sheet Pan** |
| **Chocolate** | **Slow Cooker** |
| **Dutch Oven** | **Toaster Oven** |
| **Grits** | **Tortilla** |
| **More Bacon** | **Tots** |

Each 128 pages, $9.99

Available at bookstores or directly from GIBBS SMITH
1.800.835.4993
www.gibbs-smith.com

# ABOUT THE AUTHOR

**Toni Patrick,** the culinary creative behind *101 Things To Do With Ramen Noodles* and *101 Things To Do With Mac and Cheese,* has created yet another masterpiece that makes quick work of canned biscuits. Toni has been featured on the Food Network's show *Unwrapped* and was once named Irreverent Person of the Year by *Irreverent Magazine.* She lives in Walden, Colorado, with her dog, Buddy, and two cats, Jiminy and Cricket. Toni enjoys playing in the snow, fishing, and curling up with a good book.

www.ingramcontent.com/pod-product-compliance
Lightning Source LLC
Chambersburg PA
CBHW061536050726
47593CB00002B/803